Cowgirl Christmas

By Rae Rankin

Illustrated by J-San

Text © 2018 Rae Rankin
Illustrations © 2018 J-san Art and Rae Rankin
All rights reserved. Published by Rankin Publishing
No part of this publication may be reproduced, stored in a retrieval system, or transmitted in any form or by any means, electronic, mechanical, photocopying, recording, or otherwise, without permission of the publisher. For information regarding permission, contact raerankinauthor@gmail.com

Rankin, Rae, Cowgirl Christmas/[Text by] Rae Rankin
[Illustrations by] J-san

ISBN-13: 978-0-9994340-4-8
EBook: 978-0-9994340-5-5

Typeset in Funkydori and Filson Soft
Book design by Rae Rankin
Editors: Erin McCready and Derek Heinz

For Elizabeth

and for everyone who loves the spirit of Christmas.

I watch the clock tick closer to three,
Just a few more minutes, and then I can flee.
Dad is waiting outside in his truck,
Vacation is near, but for now I am stuck.

The bell finally rings, and I race outside,
Over snow-covered sidewalks, I try not to slide.
I tug open the door and throw in my books,
Am met right away with one of Dad's famous looks.

We head out of town, over snow-covered hills,
To the barn where I ride, all is quiet and still.

Tonight, we gather to spread Christmas cheer,
To family and friends and all we hold dear.

A snowball comes whizzing fast through the air,
Splat on my cheek it appears from nowhere.
I see Dana as she races by,
I grab up some snow and let it fly.

Miss Valerie appears, holding gifts tied up with bows,
We've collected these gifts at our many horse shows.
Into Dad's truck, the presents we load,
Carefully and quickly, we get them all stowed.

The horses are warm and out of the snow,
Chores must be done, and then we can go.
Muck out the stalls, water, and feed,
Sweep out the barn, and straighten the leads.

Duchess is prancing about in her stall,
Excited and ready for a yuletide ball.
We hang up a wreath and a stocking or two,
Add red and green lights for a bright, shiny hue.

We lead out the horses and tack them on up.
Grab our warm gloves, and get a leg-up.
Led by Miss Valerie, we make our way down,
To a spot we have chosen, just out of town.

We ride out through the softly falling snow,
Bringing presents and joy to those that we know.
In his truck, Dad follows closely behind,
We hand out presents of every kind.

A crowd gathers close, their voices join flight,
Together we harmonize a sweet "Silent Night."

Back at the barn, Mom has tasty treats,
Hot chocolate and all kinds of sweets.
A quick little sip warms up my cold nose,
The warmth spreads gradually down to my toes.

We giggle and laugh, and play party games,
Taking silly pictures in a giant photo frame.
We share Christmas stories and sing some more too,
Exchange homemade gifts held together with glue.

Duchess sniffs my pocket; her treat is tucked there,
And whinnies at me in hopes I will share.
I pull out a candy cane; she takes it from me,
Then chomps it up, as content as can be!

Before we know it, our party is done,
We clean up the barn and hug everyone.
We head back home, back down from the hill.
Snowflakes drift softly, all is quiet and still.

Good night, Y'all, it's been a great night
Making peoples' lives cheery and bright.
I've hung up my stocking; I'm hitting the hay
For tomorrow brings another Cowgirl Christmas day.

Merry Christmas!

About the Author

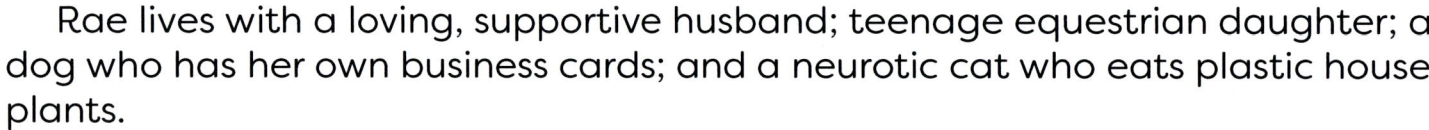

Rae is an independent marketing and graphic design consultant transplanted from sunny central California to the wilds of Utah. After two landlocked years (no the Great Salt Lake is not a substitute), her family was transferred to the Pacific Northwest. Four years later, they came full circle back to California.

Rae has always had a passion for writing and reading. *Cowgirl Christmas* is her third children's book. Her first book, *Cowgirl Lessons*, has been called a book of love and heart and her second book *Beach Day*, makes you want to hop in your car and head to the beach.

Rae lives with a loving, supportive husband; teenage equestrian daughter; a dog who has her own business cards; and a neurotic cat who eats plastic house plants.

She can be contacted at:
www.raerankin.com
http://www.facebook.com/raerankin

About the Illustrator

J-san is an illustrator and university student from Lima, Perú. He has two webcomics, *Boys and Girls* and *Ravindel*, published in Webtoon and Tapastic. J-san is also the illustrator of *Cowgirl Lessons* and *Beach Day* by Rae Rankin.

He can be contacted at:
https://www.facebook.com/jsanarte